STRUM IT GUITAR

AUTHENTIC CHORDS
ORIGINAL KEYS
COMPLETE SONGS

Jim Croce
CLASSIC HITS

Photo by Paul Wilson
Arranged by Jeff Schofield

ISBN 0-634-02735-2

HAL•LEONARD® CORPORATION

7777 W. BLUEMOUND RD. P.O. BOX 13819 MILWAUKEE, WI 53213

Visit Hal Leonard Online at
www.halleonard.com
www.croces.com

HOW TO USE THIS BOOK

Strum It™ is the series designed especially to get you playing (and singing!) along with your favorite songs. The idea is simple—the songs are arranged using their original keys in *lead sheet* format, giving you the chords for each song, beginning to end. The melody and lyrics are also shown to help you keep your spot and sing along.

Rhythm slashes are written above the staff as an accompaniment suggestion. Strum the chords in the rhythm indicated. Use the chord diagrams found at the top of the first page of the arrangement for the appropriate chord voicings.

Additional Musical Definitions

⊓	• Downstroke
∨	• Upstroke
D.S. al Coda	• Go back to the sign (𝄋), then play until the measure marked *"To Coda,"* then skip to the section labelled *"Coda."*
D.C. al Fine	• Go back to the beginning of the song and play until the measure marked *"Fine"* (end).
cont. rhy. sim.	• Continue using similar rhythm pattern.
N.C.	• Instrument is silent (drops out).
𝄆 𝄇	• Repeat measures between signs.
1. 2.	• When a repeated section has different endings, play the first ending only the first time and the second ending only the second time.

Box Number 10

Words and Music by Jim Croce

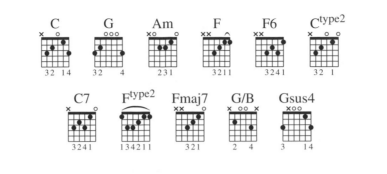

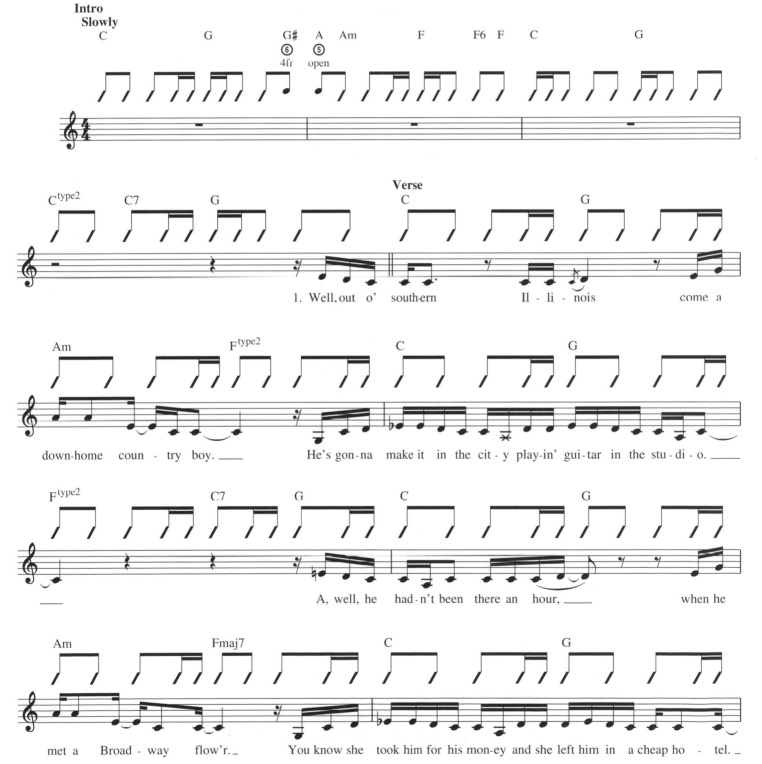

Verse

2. A, well, it's eas-y for you to see _____ that that coun-

-try boy ___ is me. _____ I'm say-in' how'm I gon-na ev-er break the news to the folks back ___ home. ___

_____ Well, I was gon-na be a great suc-cess; ___ things sure end-

-ed up ___ a mess. _____ But in the pro-cess I got messed ___ up too. ___

S Chorus

_____ But, hel - lo ma-ma and dad, ___ I had to call col-lect, 'cause I

ain't got a cent ___ to my name. ___ Well, I'm sleep-in' in the ho-tel door - way and to-

night they say it's gon-na rain. _____ And if ___ you'd on - ly send ___ me some mon-ey, I'd be

back on my feet a - gain. ___   Send it in care of the Sun - day Mis - sion,

To Coda ⊕

Box num - ber ten. ___

Verse

3. Well, back in South - ern   Il - li - nois,   they're still

worry - 'n'   'bout _ their   boy. _   But this boy's __ go - in' home soon's he gets the fare. _

Be - cause as   soon as I got __ my bread, ___   I got a

pipe up - side _ my head. ___   You know they left me in an al - ley, took my mon - ey and my gui - tar __ too. _

D.S. al Coda   ⊕ **Coda**

___   But, hel - lo,

Age

Words and Music by Jim Croce and Ingrid Croce

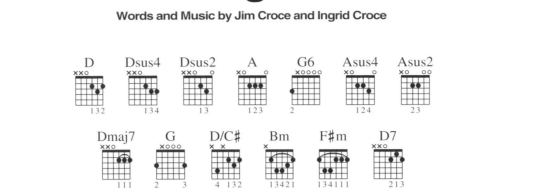

Intro
Moderately

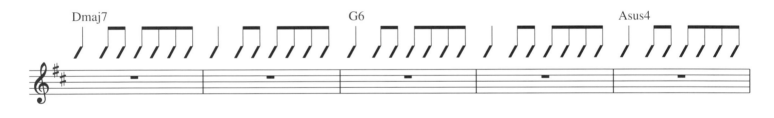

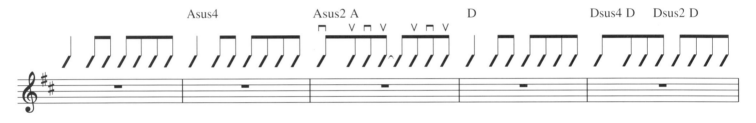

1. I've been up and down and a-round and 'round _ and back a-gain. _ I've

been so man-y plac - es I can't re-mem - ber _____ where _ or when. _ And my _

on-ly boss _ was the clock on the wall and my on-ly friend _

nev-er real-ly was _ a friend _ at all. ___ I've

𝄋 Chorus

trad-ed love for pen-nies; sold my soul _ for less. _ Lost my i-deals in that

long tun-nel of time. _ And I've turned in-side out and a-

round a-bout _ and back and then _ I found my-self _

To Coda 1 𝄌

right back where _ I start-ed _ a-gain. _

𝄋𝄋 Verse

2. Once I had my-self a mil-lion, now I've on-ly got _ a dime, _
   3. *See additional lyrics*

7

_the dif-f'rence don't _ seem quite as bad _ to - day. _ With a

_nick-el or a mil - lion, I was search-ing all _ the time _ for

To Coda 2

D.S. al Coda 1

some-thing that I nev-er lost _ or left be - hind. _ Well, I've

Coda 1

Interlude

Additional Lyrics

3. Well, now I'm in my second circle
   And I'm headin' for the top,
   I've learned a lot of things along the way.
   I'll be careful while I'm climbin'
   'Cause it hurts a lot to drop,
   And when you're down nobody gives a damn anyway.

Bad, Bad Leroy Brown

Words and Music by Jim Croce

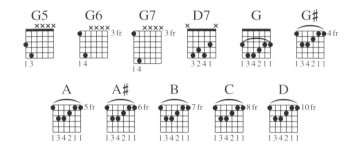

1. Well, the south - side of Chi-ca - go is the bad - dest part of town. _ And if you

3. *See additional lyrics*

go down there _ you bet-ter just be - ware _ of a man, _ name of Le-roy Brown. _ Now Le-

- roy more than trou - ble. You see he stand a-bout six foot _ four; _ all the down-

Outro-Chorus

___ bad Le-roy Brown, _ the bad-dest man _ in the whole damned town; _

bad-der than old _ King Kong ___ and mean-er than a junk-yard dog. _ And he's bad, _

(Bad.) bad (Bad.) Le-roy Brown, _ the bad-dest man _ in the whole damned town; _

bad-der than old _ King Kong ___ and mean-er than a junk-yard dog. _ Yeah, you were

bad-der than old _ King Kong ___ and mean-er than a junk-yard _ dog. _

Additional Lyrics

3. Well, Friday 'bout a week ago Leroy shootin' dice
And at the edge of the bar sat a girl name of Doris
And ooh, that girl looked nice.
Well, he cast his eyes upon her, and the trouble soon began.
And Leroy Brown, he learned a lesson 'bout a-messin' with
The wife of a jealous man.

Careful Man

Words and Music by Jim Croce

I don't gam-

ble, I don't fight, ___ I don't be hang-in' in the bars at night ___

___ Yeah, I used ___ to be a fight-er, but now ___ I am a wis-er man.

I don't drink _ much, I don't smoke, _ I don't be

hard-ly mess a-round with no dope._____ Yeah, I used ___ to be a prob-lem, but now _

_____ I am a care-ful man. Well, if you

𝄋 Bridge

used to wan-na see a com-mo-tion, you should-'ve seen the man that I used to be. _

_____ I was trou - ble in per-pet-u-al mo - tion,

trou-ble with a cap-i-tal "T". _ Stay-in' out ___ late, hav-in' fun; ___ done shot off

ev-'ry sin-gle shot in my gun._____ Yeah, I used ___ to be a lov-er, but now _
Yeah, I used ___ to be a ter-ror, but now _

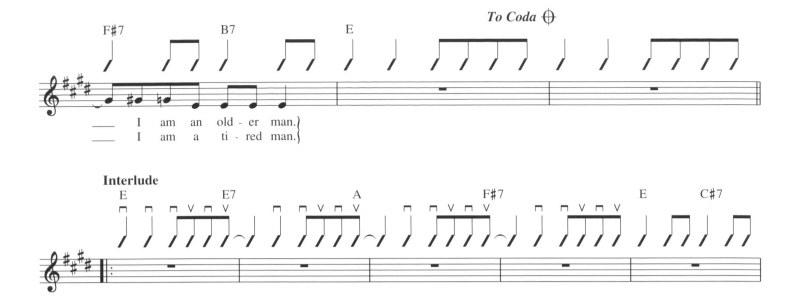

I am an old-er man.
I am a ti-red man.

Interlude

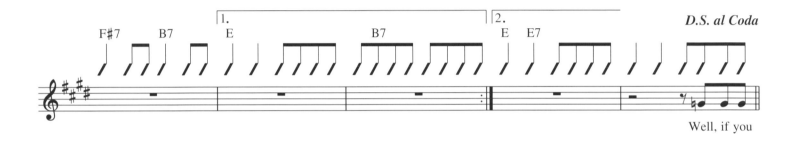

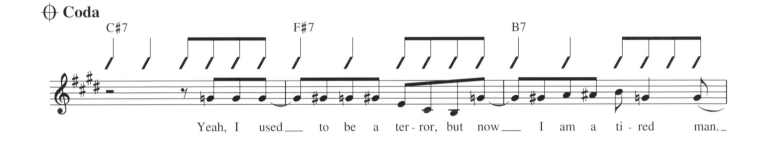

Well, if you

Coda

Yeah, I used to be a ter-ror, but now I am a ti-red man.

Outro

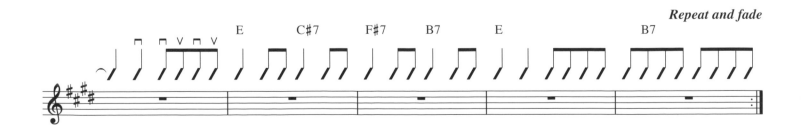

Hey Tomorrow

Words and Music by Jim Croce

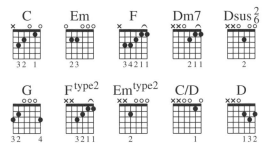

Hard Time Losin' Man

Words and Music by Jim Croce

Verse

3. Oh, Fri-day night, _ feel-in' right, _ I head out on _ the street.

Stand-in' in the _ door - way a was a deal - er known _ as Pete.

But he sold _ me a dime of some of su-per fine dy - na-mite from Mex-i - co. _

_ I spent all _ that night _ just try'n' _ to get right _ on a

Outro-Chorus

ounce of o-reg-a-no. Woo! Well, you think you've seen trou-ble, well, you're look-in' at the

man. _ Ah, _ ha. _ Oh, the world's own o-rig-i-nal hard _

Repeat and fade

_ luck sto-ry and a hard time los-in' man. Well, you think you've seen

23

I'll Have to Say I Love You in a Song

Words and Music by Jim Croce

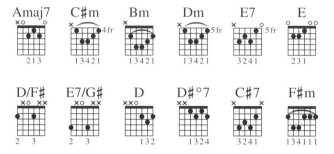

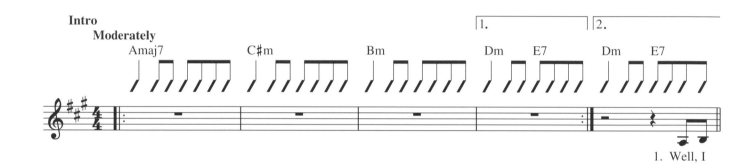

Mississippi Lady

Words and Music by Jim Croce

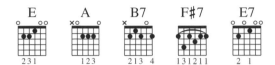

Intro
Moderately

1. Just a

℗ Verse

sleep-ing __ bag __ and an old gui - tar, I left the band in __ New Or - leans. __
2., 3. *See additional lyrics*

Did some time with the bot-tle, and some with the riv - er queens. __

Additional Lyrics

2. Hot July in Gulfport
   And I was working in the bars.
   She was working on the street
   With the rest of the evening stars.
   She said, "I never met a guy
   Who could turn my head around."
   And that's really sayin' something,
   Sweet Cordelia Brown.

3. Now I'm back in New York City,
   Playin' in a band.
   But my mind's on Mississippi,
   Is it hard to understand?
   Never thought I would meet a girl
   Who could bring me that far down.
   Like the girl I met in Gulfport,
   Sweet Cordelia Brown.

One Less Set of Footsteps

Words and Music by Jim Croce

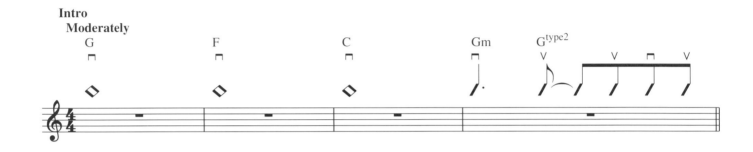

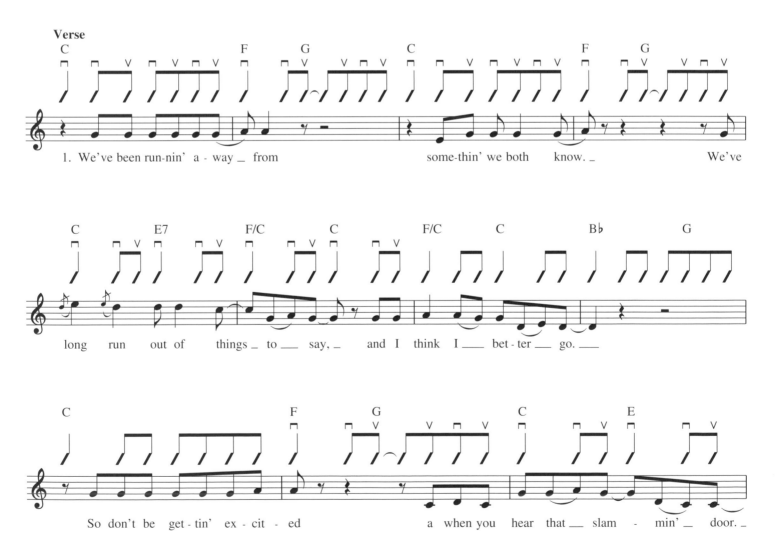

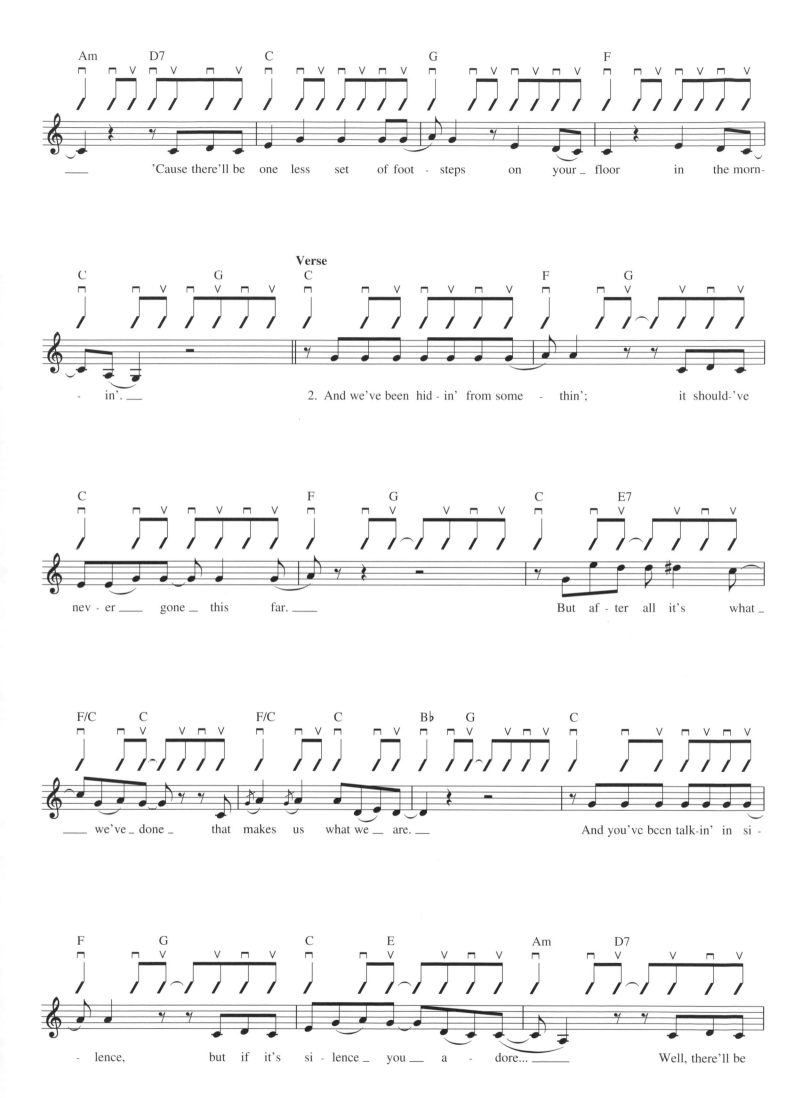

one less set of foot - steps on your floor in the morn - in'. ___ Well, there'll be

𝄋 Bridge

one less set of foot - steps on ___ your floor, ___ one less man to walk ___ in,

one less pair of jeans ___ up - on ___ your door, ___ one less voice ___ a - talk - in'. _____

Verse

___ 3., 4. But to-mor-row's a dream a - way; { mm, _ to - day has turned to dust. _ / and to - day has turned to dust. _ }

Your sil - ver tongue has turned _ to clay _ and your gold - en ___ rule _ to rust. _

If that's the way that you want ___ it, well, that's the way I ___ want _ it ___ more.

Operator
(That's Not the Way It Feels)

Words and Music by Jim Croce

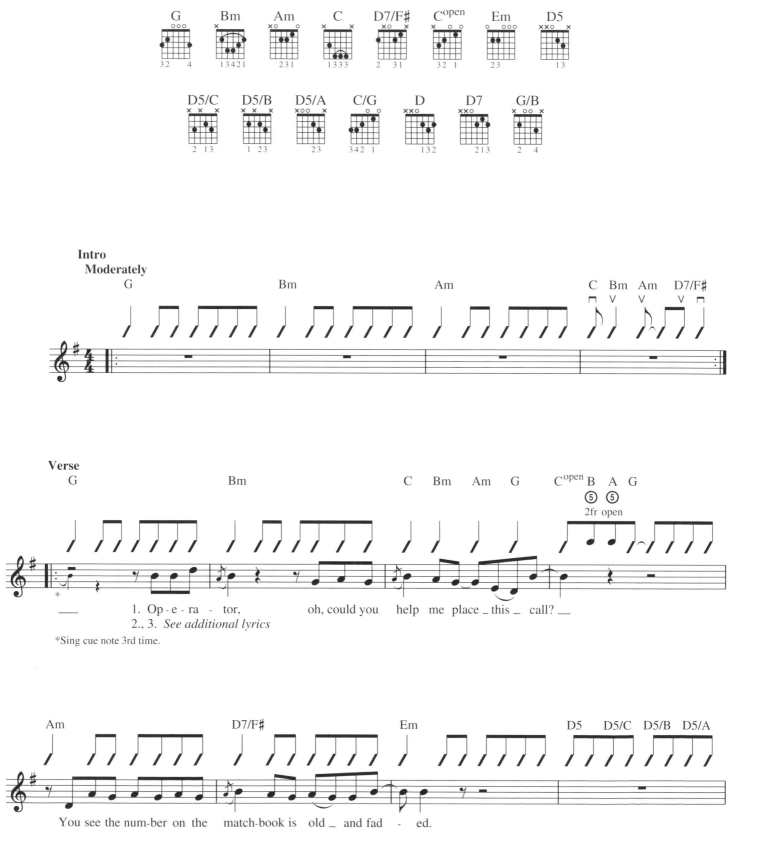

*Sing cue note 3rd time.

Additional Lyrics

2. Operator, oh could you help me place this call?
   'Cause I can't read the number that you just gave me.
   There's something in my eyes,
   You know it happens ev'ry time;
   I think about the love that I thought would save me.

3. Operator, oh let's forget about this call.
   There's no one there I really wanted to talk to.
   Thank you for your time.
   Oh, you've been so much more than kind.
   You can keep the dime.

Photographs and Memories

Words and Music by Jim Croce

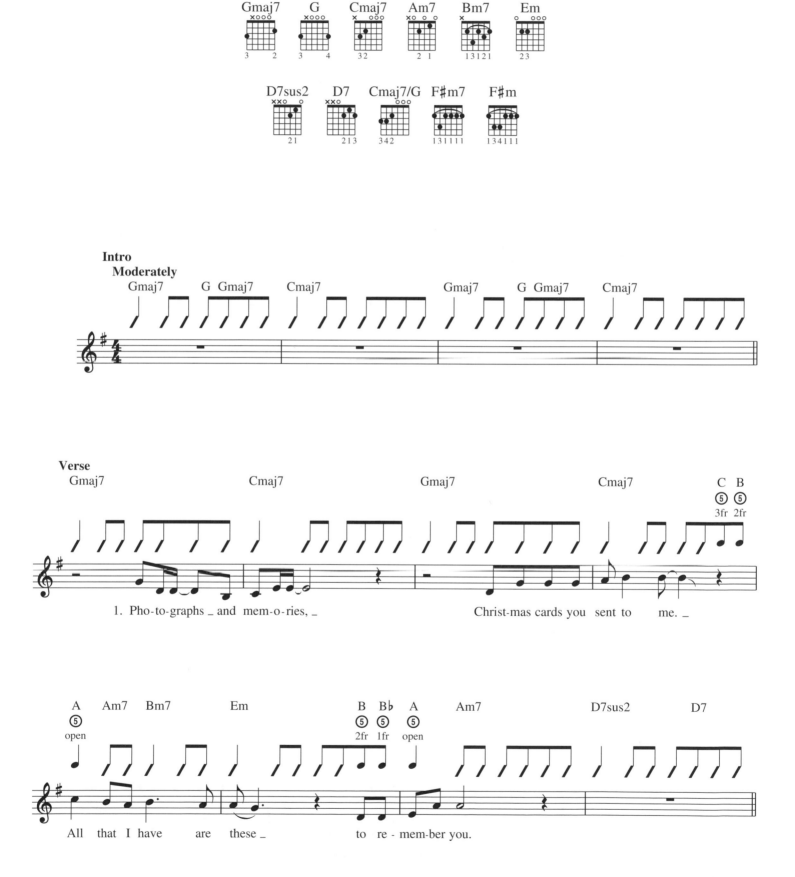

Rapid Roy
(The Stock Car Boy)

Words and Music by Jim Croce

Additional Lyrics

2. Oh, Rapid Roy that stock car boy,
   He the best driver in the land.
   He say that he learned to race a stock car
   By runnin' 'shine outa Alabam'.
   Oh, the Demolition Derby and the figure eight
   Is easy money in the bank,
   Compared to runnin' from the man in Oklahoma City
   With a five hundred gallon tank.

4. Yeah, Roy's so cool, that racin' fool,
   He don't know what fear's about,
   He do a hundred thirty mile an hour
   Smilin' at the cam'ra with a toothpick in his mouth.
   He got a girl back home name of Dixie Dawn
   But he got honeys all along the way,
   And you oughta hear them screamin' for the dirt track demon
   In a fifty-seven Chevrolet.

Roller Derby Queen

Words and Music by Jim Croce

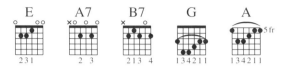

_____ my ___ hat, _____ when she caught my eye, _ and I put it back; _ and I

or-dered my - self _ coup - le o' more shots and _ beers. _

1. The night that
2., 3. You know that

Chorus

I fell in love _ with a Roll - er Der - by ___ Queen. ___ A-round 'n' 'round, a -

- round 'n' 'round. The mean-est hunk o' wom-an that an - y-bod-y ev - er seen _

To Coda ⊕ |1. ||2.

_____ down in the a - re - na. 2. She was down in the a - re - na. _____

Guitar Solo

___ ('Round 'n' 'round, a - round 'n' 'round. 'Round 'n' 'round, a - round 'n' 'round.

'Round 'n' 'round.)

3. Well, I could

Coda

Outro

down in the a - re - na. ('Round 'n' 'round, a - round 'n' 'round.

'Round 'n' 'round, a - round 'n' 'round.

Repeat and fade

'Round 'n' 'round.)

Additional Lyrics

2. She was five-foot-six and two-fifteen,
   A bleach blonde bomber with a streak of mean;
   She knew how to knuckle and she knew how to scuffle and fight.
   And the Roller Derby program said that she were
   Built like a 'frigerator with a head;
   The fans called her "Tuffy," but all her buddies called her "Spike."

3. Well, I could not help it but to fall in love
   With this heavy duty woman I been speakin' of;
   Things looked kind of bad until the day she skated into my life.
   Well, she might be nasty, she might be fat,
   But I never met a person who would tell her that.
   She's my bleach blonde bomber, my heavy handed Hackensack Mama.

Speedball Tucker

Words and Music by Jim Croce

broke-down _ rig _ on "may pop" tires, for-ty foot of o-ver-load.

2., 3. *See additional lyrics*

lot of peo-ple say that I'm cra - zy, be-cause I don't know how to take it slow. _

_ I got a broom-stick on the throt-tle, I got her

Additional Lyrics

2. You know the rain may blow, the snow may snow,
   And the turnpikes they may freeze.
   But they don't bother old Speedball,
   He goin' any damn where he please.
   He got a broomstick on the throttle,
   To keep his throttle foot a-dancin' 'round;
   With a cupful of cold black coffee
   And a pocket full of "West Coast turnarounds."

3. One day I looked into my rear-view mirror,
   And comin' up from behind
   There was a Georgia State policeman,
   A, and a hundred dollar fine.
   Well, he looked me in the eye as he was writin' me up,
   He said, "Driver, you've been flyin'.
   And ninety-five is the route you were on;
   It was not the speed limit sign."

Spin, Spin, Spin

Words and Music by Jim Croce and Ingrid Croce

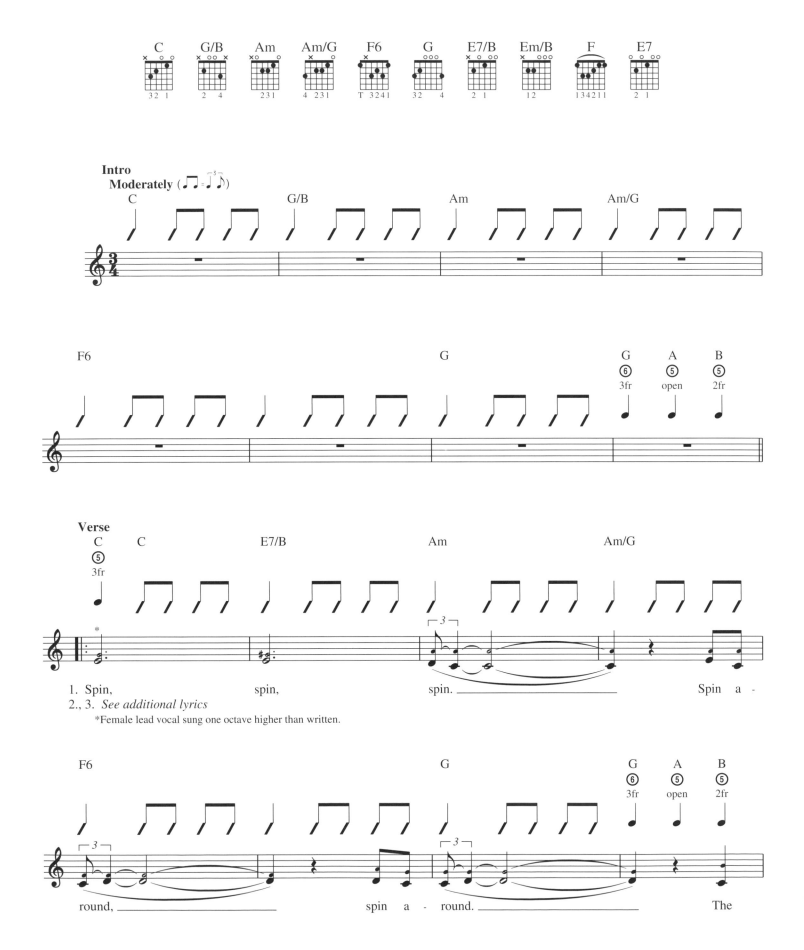

1. Spin,   spin,   spin. _____   Spin a-
2., 3. *See additional lyrics*

   *Female lead vocal sung one octave higher than written.

round, _____   spin a - round. _____   The

that life is for liv-in', that it is-n't _____ a

1., 2.

show? _____

3.

show? _____

Outro-Verse

1., 3., 4. Spin,   spin,   spin. _____ Spin a-

2. Spin,   spin,   spin. _____ Spin a-

Repeat and fade

round, _____ spin a - round. _____

way, _____ spin a - way. _____

Additional Lyrics

2. Spin, spin, spin.
   Spin around, spin around.
   You look out on the city from your penthouse so high.
   Spin around.
   But your pedestal's your prison and so is your high.
   Spin around.
   But where are you spinnin', and when will you know
   That life is for livin', that it isn't a show?

3. Spin, spin, spin.
   Spin around, spin around.
   Your pills are your conscience, they make ev'rything seem alright.
   Spin around.
   Take a white one to go to sleep, take a red one to stay up all night
   To spin around.
   But where are you spinnin', and when will you know
   That life is for livin', that it isn't a show.

Workin' at the Car Wash Blues

Words and Music by Jim Croce

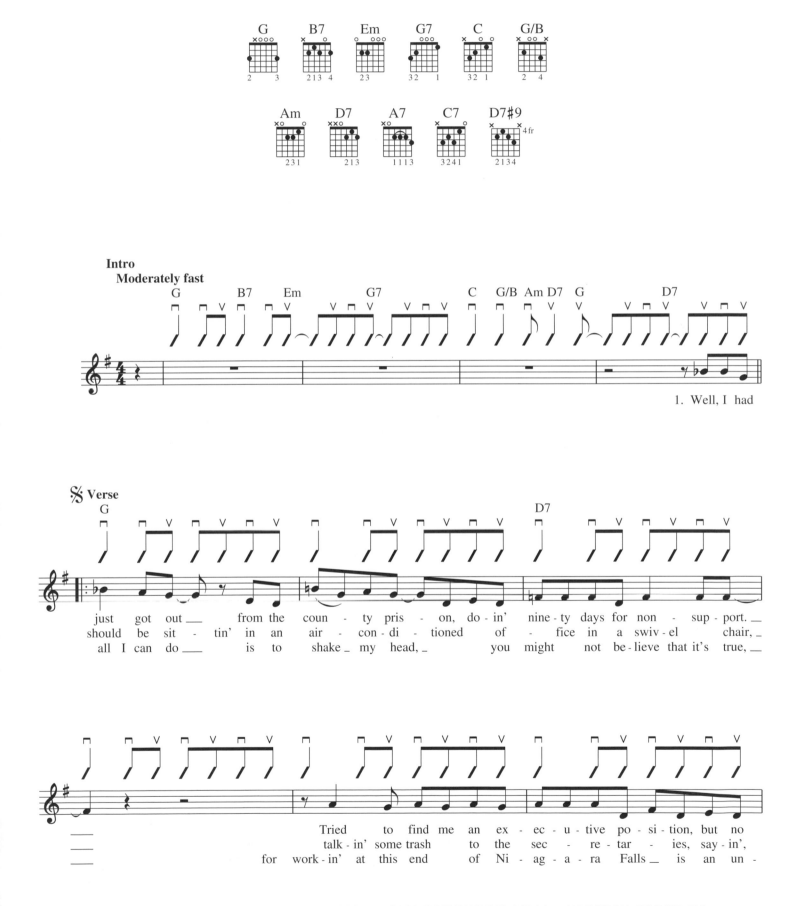

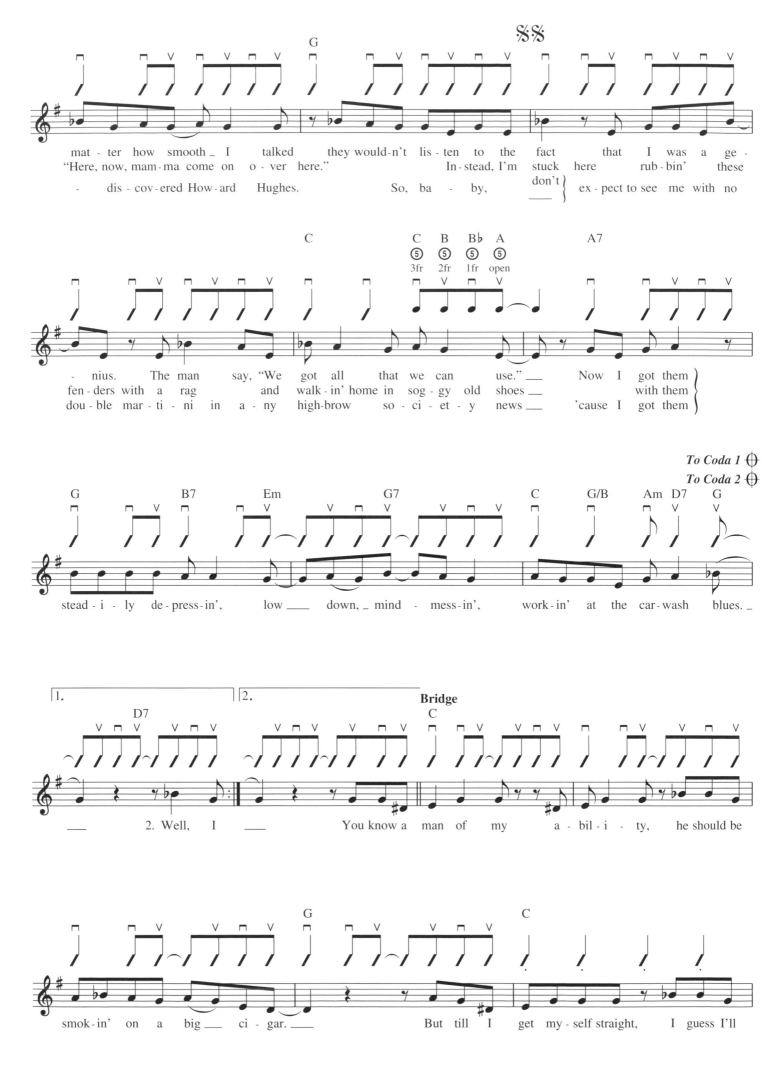

just have to wait in my rub-ber suit a rub-bin' these cars. ____ 3. Well,

Coda 1

Interlude

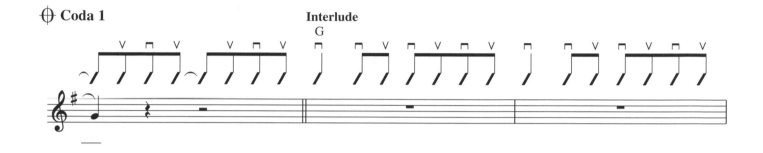

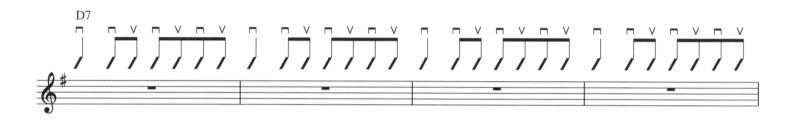

D.S.S. al Coda 2
(3rd lyrics)

Coda 2

So, ba-by, don't ____ ____ Yeah, I got them

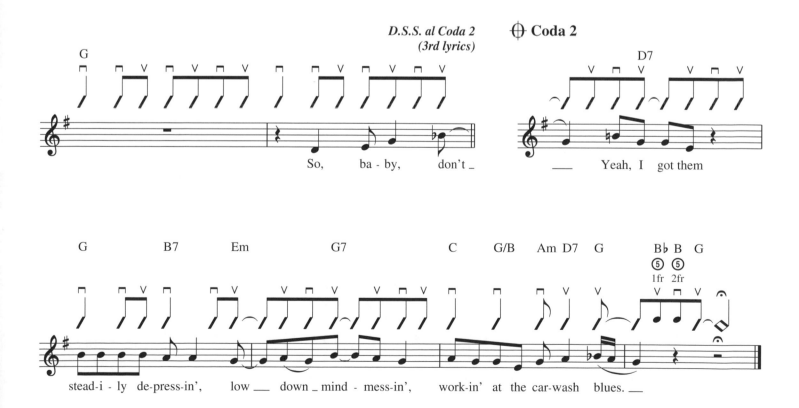

stead-i-ly de-press-in', low ___ down ___ mind-mess-in', work-in' at the car-wash blues. ____

Time in a Bottle

Words and Music by Jim Croce

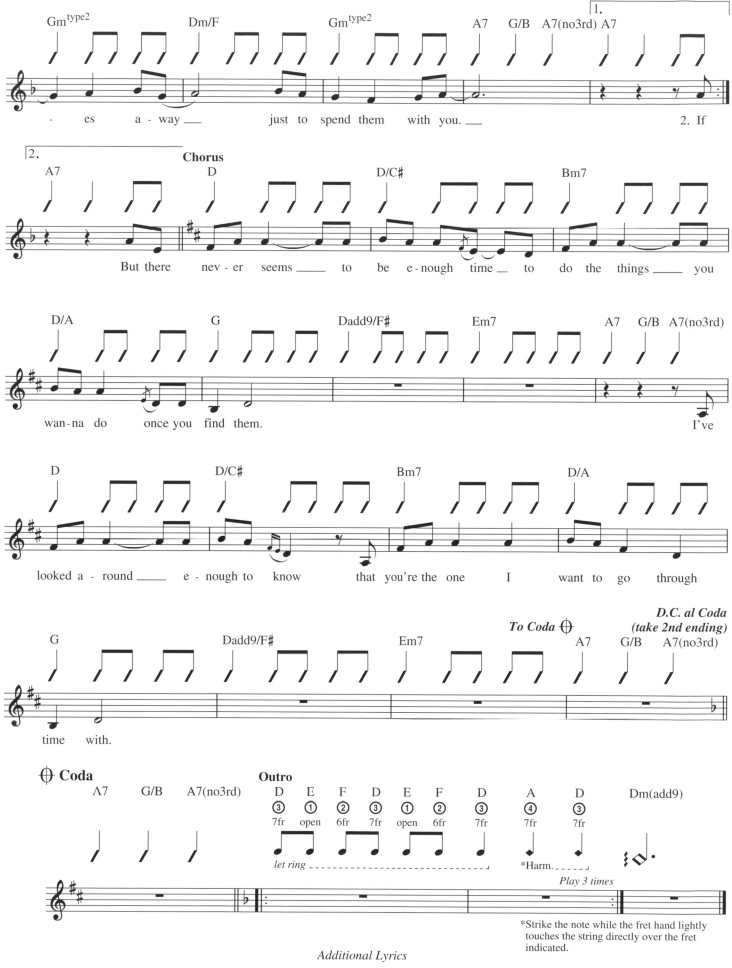

Additional Lyrics

2. If I could make days last forever,
   If words could make wishes come true;
   I'd save ev'ry day like a treasure and then,
   Again I would spend them with you.

3. If I had a box just for wishes,
   And dreams that had never come true;
   The box would be empty except for mem'ry of
   How they were answered by you.

Tomorrow's Gonna Be a Brighter Day

Words and Music by Jim Croce

make you a chain out of dia - monds, _ and pearls from a sum - mer sea. _____ But

all I can give you is a kiss in the morn - in' and a sweet a - pol - o - gy.

2. Well, I know that it has - n't been eas - y and I
3. *See additional lyrics*

have - n't al - ways been a - round; _ to say the right words, or to hold you in the morn - in', or to

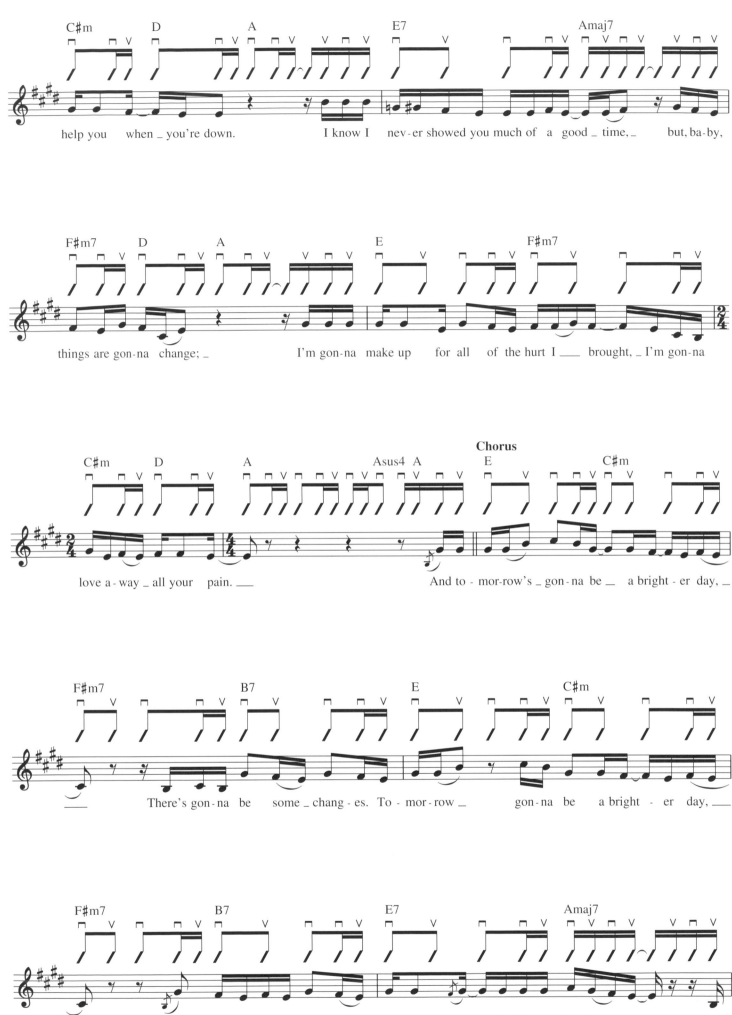

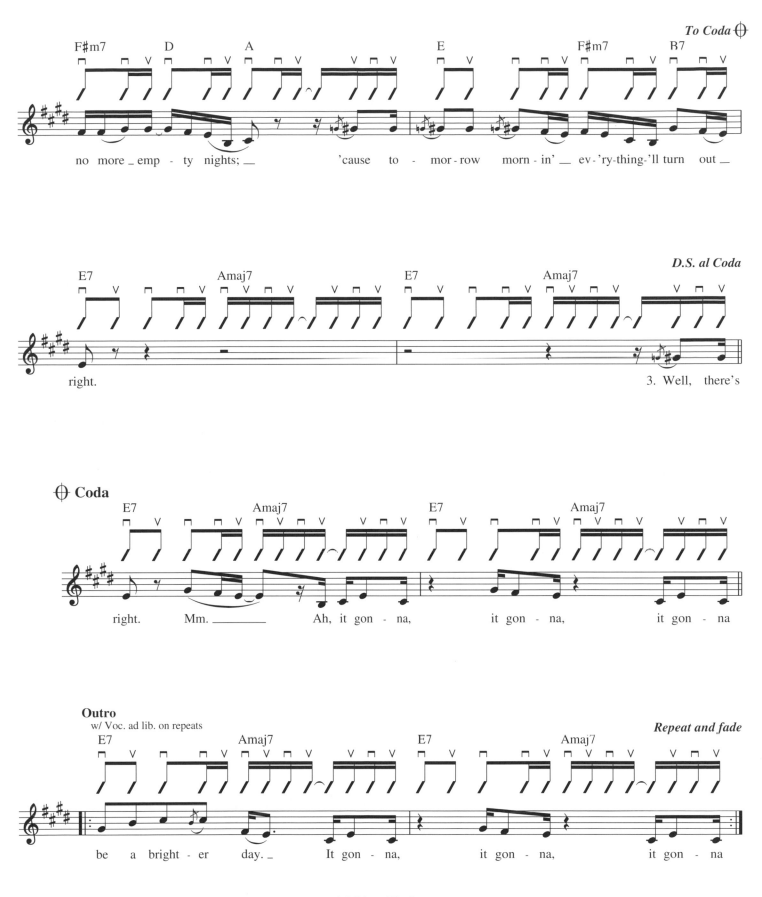

Additional Lyrics

3. Well, there's something that I gotta tell you,
Yes, I got something on my mind;
But words come hard when you're lyin' in my arms,
And when I'm lookin' deep into your eyes.
But there's truth and consolation
In what I'm tryin' to say;
Is that nobody ever had a rainbow, baby,
Until he had the rain.

You Don't Mess Around With Jim

Words and Music by Jim Croce

cape. You don't spit in-to the wind. _ You don't pull the mask off the

old Lone Rang - er and you don't mess a-round with _ Jim." _ A doo, doo, da, da,

dee, dee, dee, dee, dee, dee.

Verse

2. Well, out-ta South Al - a-bam - a come a
3. *See additional lyrics*

cont. rhy. sim.

coun-try boy. He said, "I'm look-in' for a man named Jim, ___ I am a

pool shoot-in' boy, my name is Wil-lie Mc-Coy _ but down home they call me Slim. _ Yeah, I'm look-

- in' for the King of For-ty - sec-ond Street, he driv-in' a drop - top Cad-il-lac.

Additional Lyrics

3. Well, a hush fell over the poolroom,
   Jimmy come boppin' in off the street.
   And when the cuttin' were done,
   The only part that wasn't bloody was
   The soles of the big man's feet. Woo!
   Yeah, he were cut in 'bout a hundred places,
   And he were shot in a couple more.
   And you better believe they sung a diff'rent kind of story
   When a big Jim hit the floor.
   Oh. Now they say you don't...

· AUTHENTIC CHORDS · ORIGINAL KEYS · COMPLETE SONGS ·

The *Strum It* series lets players strum the chords and sing along with their favorite hits. Each song has been selected because it can be played with regular open chords, barre chords, or other moveable chord types. Guitarists can simply play the rhythm, or play and sing along through the entire song. All songs are shown in their original keys complete with chords, strum patterns, melody and lyrics. Wherever possible, the chord voicings from the recorded versions are notated.

Acoustic Classics
00699238 / $10.95
21 classics: And I Love Her • Barely Breathing • Free Fallin' • Maggie May • Mr. Jones • Only Wanna Be with You • Patience • Wonderful Tonight • Yesterday • more.

The Beach Boys' Greatest Hits
00699357/ $12.95
19 tunes: Barbara Ann • California Girls • Fun, Fun, Fun • Good Vibrations • Help Me Rhonda • I Get Around • Surfer Girl • Surfin' U.S.A. • Wouldn't It Be Nice • more.

The Beatles Favorites
00699249 / $14.95
23 Beatles hits: Can't Buy Me Love • Eight Days a Week • Hey Jude • Let It Be • She Loves You • Yesterday • You've Got to Hide Your Love Away • and more.

Best of Contemporary Christian
00699531 / $12.95
20 CCM favorites: Awesome God • Butterfly Kisses • El Shaddai • Father's Eyes • I Could Sing of Your Love Forever • Jesus Freak • The Potter's Hand • and more.

Best of Steven Curtis Chapman
00699530 / $12.95
16 top hits: For the Sake of the Call • Heaven in the Real World • His Strength Is Perfect • I Will Be Here • More to This Life • Signs of Life • What Kind of Joy • more.

Very Best of Johnny Cash
00699514 / $9.95
17 songs: A Boy Named Sue • Daddy Sang Bass • Folsom Prison Blues • I Walk the Line • The Man in Black • Orange Blossom Special • Ring of Fire • and more.

Celtic Guitar Songbook
00699265 / $9.95
35 songs: Cockles and Mussels • Danny Boy • The Irish Washerwoman • Kerry Dance • Killarney • My Wild Irish Rose • Sailor's Hornpipe • and more.

Christmas Songs for Guitar
00699247 / $9.95
40 favorites: Frosty the Snow Man • Grandma Got Run Over by a Reindeer • I'll Be Home for Christmas • Rockin' Around the Christmas Tree • Silver Bells • more.

Christmas Songs with 3 Chords
00699487 / $8.95
30 all-time favorites: Angels We Have Heard on High • Away in a Manger • Here We Come A-Wassailing • Jolly Old St. Nicholas • Silent Night • Up on the Housetop • more.

Very Best of Eric Clapton
00699560 / $12.95
20 songs: Change the World • For Your Love • I Shot the Sheriff • Layla • My Father's Eyes • Tears in Heaven • White Room • Wonderful Tonight • and more.

Country Strummin'
00699119 / $8.95
Features 24 songs: Achy Breaky Heart • Blue • A Broken Wing • Gone Country • I Fall to Pieces • She and I • Unchained Melody • What a Crying Shame • and more.

Jim Croce – Classic Hits
00699269 / $10.95
22 great songs: Bad, Bad Leroy Brown • I'll Have to Say I Love You in a Song • Operator (That's Not the Way It Feels) • Time in a Bottle • and more.

Very Best of John Denver
00699488 / $12.95
20 top hits: Leaving on a Jet Plane • Rocky Mountain High • Sunshine on My Shoulders • Take Me Home, Country Roads • Thank God I'm a Country Boy • more.

Neil Diamond
00699593 / $12.95
28 classics: America • Cracklin' Rosie • Forever in Blue Jeans • Hello Again • I'm a Believer • Love on the Rocks • Song Sung Blue • Sweet Caroline • and more.

Disney Favorites
00699171 / $10.95
34 Disney favorites: Can You Feel the Love Tonight • Cruella De Vil • Friend Like Me • It's a Small World • Under the Sea • Whistle While You Work • and more.

Disney Greats
00699172 / $10.95
39 classics: Beauty and the Beast • Colors of the Wind • Go the Distance • Heigh-Ho • Kiss the Girl • When You Wish Upon a Star • Zip-A-Dee-Doo-Dah • and more.

Best of The Doors
00699177 / $10.95
25 Doors favorites: Been Down So Long • Hello I Love You Won't You Tell Me Your Name? • Light My Fire • Riders on the Storm • Touch Me • and more.

Favorite Songs with 3 Chords
00699112 / $8.95
27 popular songs: All Shook Up • Boot Scootin' Boogie • Great Balls of Fire • Lay Down Sally • Semi-Charmed Life • Twist and Shout • Wooly Bully • and more.

Favorite Songs with 4 Chords
00699270 / $8.95
22 tunes: Beast of Burden • Don't Be Cruel • Gloria • I Fought the Law • La Bamba • Last Kiss • Let Her Cry • Love Stinks • Peggy Sue • 3 AM • Wild Thing • and more.

Fireside Sing-Along
00699273 / $8.95
25 songs: Edelweiss • Leaving on a Jet Plane • Take Me Home, Country Roads • Teach Your Children • This Land Is Your Land • You've Got a Friend • and more.

Folk Favorites
00699517 / $8.95
42 traditional favorites: Camptown Races • Clementine • Danny Boy • My Old Kentucky Home • Rock-A-My Soul • Scarborough Fair • and more.

Irving Berlin's God Bless America®
00699508 / $9.95
25 patriotic anthems: America, the Beautiful • Battle Hymn of the Republic • God Bless America • The Star Spangled Banner • This Land Is Your Land • and more.

Great '50s Rock
00699187 / $9.95
28 hits: At the Hop • Blueberry Hill • Bye Bye Love • Hound Dog • Rock Around the Clock • That'll Be the Day • and more.

Great '60s Rock
00699188 / $9.95
27 classic rock songs: And I Love Her • Gloria • Mellow Yellow • Return to Sender • Runaway • Surfin' U.S.A. • The Twist • Under the Boardwalk • Wild Thing • more.

Great '70s Rock
00699262 / $9.95
21 classic hits: Band on the Run • Lay Down Sally • Let It Be • Love Hurts • Ramblin' Man • Time for Me to Fly • Two Out of Three Ain't Bad • Wild World • and more.

Great '80s Rock
00699263 / $9.95
23 favorites: Centerfold • Free Fallin' • Got My Mind Set on You • Kokomo • Should I Stay or Should I Go • Uptown Girl • What I Like About You • and more.

Great '90s Rock
00699268 / $9.95
17 contemporary hits: If You Could Only See • Iris • Mr. Jones • Only Wanna Be with You • Tears in Heaven • Torn • The Way • You Were Meant for Me • and more.

Best of Woody Guthrie
00699496 / $12.95
20 songs: Do Re Mi • The Grand Coulee Dam • Roll On, Columbia • So Long It's Been Good to Know Yuh • This Land Is Your Land • Tom Joad • and more.

John Hiatt Collection
00699398 / $12.95
17 classics: Angel Eyes • Feels Like Rain • Have a Little Faith in Me • Riding with the King • Thing Called Love (Are You Ready for This Thing Called Love) • and more.

Hymn Favorites
00699271 / $9.95
Includes: Amazing Grace • Down by the Riverside • Holy, Holy, Holy • Just as I Am • Rock of Ages • What a Friend We Have in Jesus • and more.

Carole King Collection
00699234 / $12.95
20 songs: I Feel the Earth Move • It's Too Late • A Natural Woman • So Far Away • Tapestry • Will You Love Me Tomorrow • You've Got a Friend • and more.

Very Best of Dave Matthews Band
00699520 / $12.95
12 favorites: Ants Marching • Crash into Me • Crush • Don't Drink the Water • Everyday • The Space Between • Stay (Wasting Time) • What Would You Say • and more.

Sarah McLachlan
00699231 / $10.95
20 of Sarah's hits: Angel • Building a Mystery • I Will Remember You • Ice Cream • Sweet Surrender • more.

A Merry Christmas Songbook
00699211 / $8.95
51 holiday hits: Away in a Manger • Deck the Hall • Fum, Fum, Fum • The Holly and the Ivy • Jolly Old St. Nicholas • O Christmas Tree • and more!

More Favorite Songs with 3 Chords
00699532 / $8.95
27 great hits: Barbara Ann • Gloria • Hang on Sloopy • Hound Dog • La Bamba • Mony, Mony • Rock Around the Clock • Rock This Town • Rockin' Robin • and more.

Pop-Rock Guitar Favorites
00699088 / $8.95
31 songs: Angie • Brown Eyed Girl • Eight Days a Week • Free Bird • Gloria • Hey Jude • Let It Be • Maggie May • Wild Thing • Wonderful Tonight • and more.

Elvis! Greatest Hits
00699276 / $10.95
24 Elvis classics: All Shook Up • Always on My Mind • Can't Help Falling in Love • Hound Dog • It's Now or Never • Jailhouse Rock • Love Me Tender • and more.

Songs for Kids
00699616 / $9.95
28 fun favorites: Alphabet Song • Bingo • Frere Jacques • Kum Ba Yah • London Bridge • Old MacDonald • Pop Goes the Weasel • Yankee Doodle • more.

Best of George Strait
00699235 / $10.95
20 Strait hits: Adalida • All My Ex's Live in Texas • Carried Away • Does Fort Worth Ever Cross Your Mind • Right or Wrong • Write This Down • and more.

25 Country Standards
00699523 / $12.95
Includes: Always on My Mind • Amazed • Elvira • Friends in Low Places • Hey, Good Lookin' • Sixteen Tons • You Are My Sunshine • Your Cheatin' Heart • and more.

Best of Hank Williams Jr.
00699224 / $10.95
24 signature standards: All My Rowdy Friends Are Coming Over Tonight • Honky Tonkin' • There's a Tear in My Beer • Whiskey Bent and Hell Bound • and more.

Women of Rock
00699183 / $9.95
22 hits: Don't Speak • Give Me One Reason • I Don't Want to Wait • Insensitive • Lovefool • Stay • Torn • You Oughta Know • You Were Meant for Me • and more.

FOR MORE INFORMATION, SEE YOUR LOCAL MUSIC DEALER, OR WRITE TO:

HAL•LEONARD® CORPORATION
7777 W. BLUEMOUND RD. P.O. BOX 13819 MILWAUKEE, WI 53213

Visit Hal Leonard online at www.halleonard.com

Prices, contents & availability subject to change without notice.

0604